Charles Dickens

Charles Dickens

Nicola Barber and Patrick Lee-Browne

This edition published in 2008 by
Evans Brothers Ltd.
2A Portman Mansions
Chiltern Street
London W1U 6NR

© Evans Brothers Limited 2008

British Library Cataloguing in Publication Data

Barber, Nicola
    Charles Dickens. - Rev. ed. - (Writers and their times)
    1. Dickens, Charles, 1812-1870 - Juvenile literature
    2. Novelists, English - 19th century - Biography - Juvenile
    literature
    I. Title II. Lee-Browne, Patrick
    823.8

ISBN-13: 9780237536480

Printed in Dubai

This book is dedicated to Set 6a5

Acknowledgements

Consultant – Dr Tony Williams

Editor – Su Swallow
Designer – Ann Samuel
Production – Jenny Mulvanny
Picture Research – Victoria Brooker

For permission to reproduce copyright material, the authors and publishers gratefully acknowledge the following:

Cover (top) Hulton Getty (bottom left) Dickens House Museum (bottom centre) Mary Evans Picture Library (bottom right) Aquarius Library **title page** Eastgate Museum, Rochester/Bridgeman Art Library **contents page** Victoria and Albert Museum/Bridgeman Art Library **page 6** (top) Dickens House Museum/Bridgeman Art Library (bottom) Dickens House Museum **page 7** (top) Victoria and Albert Museum/Bridgeman Art Library (bottom) Hulton Getty **page 8** Mary Evans Picture Library **page 9** (top) Guildhall Library, Corporation of London/Bridgeman Art Library (bottom) Hulton Getty **page 10** (top) Collections/Liz Stares (bottom) Guildhall Library, Corporation of London/Bridgeman Art Library **page 11** (top) Mary Evans Picture Library (bottom) Dickens House Museum **page 12** Dickens House Museum **page 13** (top) Mary Evans Picture Library (bottom) Mary Evans Picture Library **page 14** Mary Evans Picture Library **page 15** (top) Dickens House Museum (bottom) Mary Evans Picture Library **page 16** (top) Mary Evans Picture Library (bottom) Dickens House Museum **page 17** (top) Mary Evans Picture Library (bottom) Hulton Getty **page 18** (top) Hulton Getty (bottom) Mary Evans Picture Library **page 19** (top) BBC Photograph Library (bottom) Aquarius Library **page 20** Victoria and Albert Museum/Bridgeman Art Library **page 21** (top) Mary Evans Picture Library (bottom) Dickens House Museum **page 22** (top) Hulton Getty (bottom) Hulton Getty **page 23** (top) Mary Evans Picture Library (bottom) Hulton Getty **page 24** Aquarius Library **page 25** (top) BBC Photograph Library (bottom) Collections/Fay Godwin **page 26** (top) BBC Photograph Library (bottom) Eastgate Museum, Rochester/Bridgeman Art Library **page 27** (left) Aquarius Library (right) Dickens House Museum

Contents

Dickens's world

When he was a child, Charles Dickens used to walk with his father past a large and imposing house near to their home town of Chatham in Kent. "If you work very hard," John Dickens said to his son, "you could one day live in a house like that." Then father and son would walk homewards, to their own small, cramped home overlooking the River Medway in Chatham. The large house was Gad's Hill Place, and John Dickens's words were to come true: Charles Dickens did work extremely hard all his life, and he did eventually become the owner of Gad's Hill Place.

Charles Dickens was a phenomenal success as an author in his own lifetime, and his reputation has continued to flourish ever since. Today, he is best-known for his 15 great novels, but he was also a playwright, an accomplished actor, a theatre producer, a journalist, editor of newspapers and magazines, and a social reformer who believed passionately in practical action for the injustices and ills he saw all around him. He set nearly all of his novels in his own time, using them to highlight particular social problems such as lack of education, or the conditions in factories. His fictional characters, although not necessarily based on living people, were drawn from his acute observations of the people he saw all around him, particularly in the streets of London.

This portrait of Charles Dickens was painted when the author was 27 by his close friend, the artist Daniel Maclise (1806-70). It is known as the 'Nickleby portrait' and was said by his friends to be a very good likeness of Dickens.

Gad's Hill Place near Chatham in Kent. This was the house that Dickens saw as a child and bought as an adult. It is now a school.

The Industrial Revolution

Charles Dickens was born at a time when the effects of the Industrial Revolution were being felt across Great Britain. The Industrial Revolution is a term used to describe several changes that began in Britain after about 1760. These changes included improvements in transport and communications, the invention of steam-driven machinery, an increase in population and the growth in the size of towns.

In some areas of the country the effects of industrialisation were dramatic as mines, mills and factories opened, and canals and railways (see box) were constructed to transport goods. Before, iron and coal had been produced on a small scale in the south and west of England. Now huge iron and coalworks were opened in South Wales, the Midlands and Scotland, bringing new wealth and employment to these areas. Cloth production, traditionally centred in people's homes in East Anglia and the southwest of England, moved to the mills of Lancashire and Yorkshire. By about 1830, Britain was the first fully industrialised nation in the world.

Industry on the River Tyne in northeast England in the 19th century. The painting is by William Bell Scott (1811-90).

The power of steam

By 1800, British engineers had already discovered how to harness the power of steam to drive machinery. Throughout the early 19th century, engineers continued to improve steam-driven engines. In 1825, the Stockton-Darlington railway opened. Designed by the Scottish engineer, George Stephenson, it was used to carry coal from Darlington to the port of Stockton 32 kilometres away. Its steam-driven locomotive pulled more coal than horse-drawn carts, proving that railways could be profitable. In 1830, the Liverpool to Manchester railway opened. This railway carried passengers – one of whom described the sensation of travelling at over 45 kilometres an hour as 'really flying'! It was the beginning of the railway boom.

The impressive railway viaduct in Stockport, near Manchester, is as tall as the chimneys of the surrounding mills and factories. This railway line was built to connect London and northwest England.

Wealth and poverty

The Industrial Revolution brought more money and better living conditions for many people. But for others, life was harsh and miserable. Working conditions in many of the new factories were atrocious. Children as young as six or seven were employed in mines and factories. In the mines they crawled on hands and knees through dark, damp tunnels, dragging carts full of coal. In the factories they worked around unprotected moving machinery, and horrific accidents were quite common. Women and children often worked for 12 or 14 hours, with only one hour's break. Holidays were unheard of. The government attempted to control some of the worst abuses with various Factory Acts; for example the Act of 1833 forbade the employment of children under nine in the mills, and tried to limit the working day for 9- to 13-year-olds to nine hours.

Slum squalor

Despite the grim conditions, people continued to flock to towns and cities to work in the new mills and factories. Wages were better and more reliable than in the countryside. However, the increasing population in towns and cities presented a new set of problems. Housing for the new workforce was often overcrowded and filthy. Some houses were built around a court with just one tap and one toilet for all the inhabitants. Conditions did not begin to improve until the 1860s, when proper sewerage and drainage systems began to be installed in the capital and, later, in cities elsewhere.

A dingy slum in central London, as depicted by the French artist Gustave Doré

Parliamentary reform

In the early 1800s, Parliament was made up mainly of wealthy landowners. People who did not own property were not allowed to vote. But with the changes of the Industrial Revolution, different areas of the country became important and wealthy. Towns such as Leeds and Birmingham grew rapidly, yet they had no Member of Parliament to represent them in the House of Commons. The Reform Act of 1832 addressed this problem by giving many industrial areas their own MPs. It also allowed any man who owned property worth £10 a year or more to vote. This qualification excluded most factory workers and no women were permitted to vote.

Dickens knew for himself the evils of child labour and insanitary housing conditions. As a young man he experienced at first hand the squalor and misery of the slum areas of London. He wrote:

66 *The amount of crime, starvation and nakedness and misery of every sort in the metropolis surpasses all understanding...* 99

The workhouse

In 1834, the government passed the New Poor Law. This law was hated by those it affected, and by Dickens himself. The law stopped cash payments to anyone who was able-bodied yet unemployed unless they entered a workhouse. In the workhouse, families were separated, forced to wear workhouse clothes and kept in terrible conditions. Dickens wrote *Oliver Twist*, the tale of the workhouse boy who is foolish enough to 'ask for more', as a direct result of the 1834 law.

A workhouse in London. The workhouse was the only refuge for the very poor.

Education

As well as slum conditions, another area of great interest to Dickens was education for the poor and deprived. Most children in the early 19th century received no schooling at all. Dickens and others believed that lack of education left the ignorant and poor little choice but to turn to crime and prostitution. He saw education as one of the keys to improving the lot of the deprived. As a result he became involved with the Ragged School movement – charitable schools run by volunteers which offered basic education to poor children.

A Ragged School in Edinburgh in about 1850. The Ragged Schools offered poor children a chance of basic education.

Dickens visited one of the Ragged Schools in 1843. He was there on behalf of a wealthy heiress, Angela Burdett-Coutts (see page 23). He reported that the school was: 'held in three most wretched rooms on the first floor of a rotten house; every plank, and timber, and brick, and lath, and piece of plaster in which shakes as you walk...' Ever practical, Dickens recommended that the first priority was to provide a sink, soap and towels for the filthy children to clean themselves, and to find a less dilapidated schoolroom with better ventilation.

Charles John Huffam Dickens

Charles Dickens was born in a house on the outskirts of Portsmouth on 7 February 1812. His father worked in the Navy Pay Office at Portsmouth Dockyard, but when Charles was five years old, the family moved to Chatham. Charles was a sickly little boy who often preferred to stay indoors and read his books rather than play outside. He also loved going to the theatre – he was taken to see Christmas pantomimes in London, and was a frequent spectator at travelling fairs, and at the Theatre Royal in the neighbouring town of Rochester.

The house where Charles Dickens was born, in Old Commercial Road, Portsmouth. Today, the house is open to visitors.

The blacking factory, where the young Dickens was sent to work, stood on the Hungerford Stairs just off the Strand in London (near where Charing Cross Station stands today).

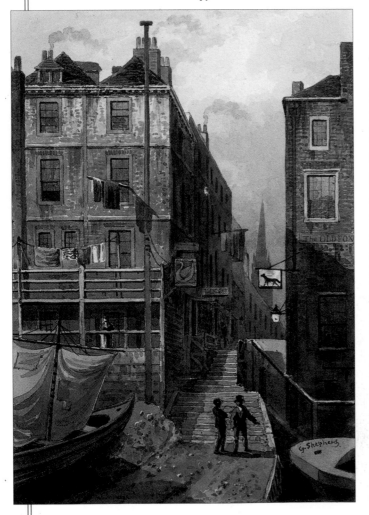

The blacking factory

In 1822, the family was on the move once more – this time to London. By this time, John Dickens had severe financial problems. He was unable to support his large family – there were now six children – and was constantly getting into debt. Although he sent Charles's elder sister, Fanny, to the Royal Academy of Music, there seemed to be no plan to continue Charles's education. The young boy had attended a school in Chatham, but now he was left to wander the unfamiliar streets of London. Charles was bewildered by the change in his circumstances – but worse was to follow. When Charles was 12 years old, a friend of the family offered to employ him in a warehouse where boot-blacking was made. Charles's job was to cover the pots of boot-blacking and to paste a label on to them. He worked from eight in the morning until eight at night, with an hour's break for dinner and half an hour for tea, for which he was paid six shillings a week. His parents needed the extra income, but Charles was in despair.

He later wrote:

> *It is wonderful to me how I could have been so easily cast away at such an age... My father and mother were quite satisfied. They could hardly have been more so, if I had been twenty years of age, distinguished at a grammar-school and going to Cambridge.*

Despite efforts to pay off his debts, in 1824 John Dickens was arrested and imprisoned in Marshalsea Prison. The rest of the family was eventually obliged to join him in the prison, except for Charles and Fanny who continued to live in their lodgings. They would visit the crowded prison every Sunday, an experience which was to be relived later on by Dickens in his novel *Little Dorrit* (see box).

In May 1824, John Dickens's mother died and left enough money for the Dickens family to be released from the Marshalsea. A short while later, John Dickens also removed his son from the blacking factory. Charles Dickens went back to school, but his experiences of both the prison and the factory stayed with him as terrible and haunting memories throughout his life.

John Dickens, father of Charles Dickens. John Dickens was always a hospitable and generous man – but as a consequence he was constantly in debt.

The Marshalsea Prison

In *Little Dorrit*, Dickens describes the Marshalsea Prison as 'an oblong pile of barrack building, partitioned into squalid houses standing back to back... environed by a narrow paved yard, hemmed in by high walls duly spiked at top'. Conditions inside are described in equally vivid detail: 'It was a hot summer day, and the prison rooms were baking between the high walls. In the debtor's confined chamber, Mrs Bangham, charwoman and messenger... had volunteered her services as fly-catcher and general attendant. The walls and ceiling were blackened with flies...'

The Marshalsea Prison was in Borough High Street, and one wall of the prison still survives.

First love and success

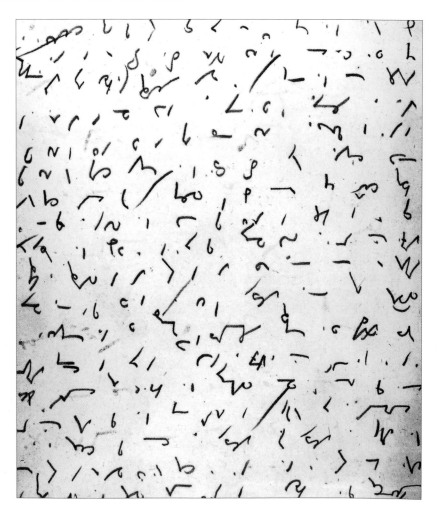

Financial difficulties struck again in 1827 and, as his parents could no longer afford the fees for his education, Charles Dickens left school for good. At the age of 15 he started his career in the adult world. His first job was in a lawyer's office, but he found the work very dull and was soon looking out for new possibilities. His father had recently learned shorthand and taken a new job as a parliamentary reporter. Charles decided to follow his example and started to teach himself shorthand – a slow and tedious process. However, his hard work paid off. In 1831 he became a parliamentary reporter for the *Mirror of Parliament* and, the following year, a general reporter for a new paper *The True Sun*. He was soon to have a reputation as the quickest and most accurate shorthand reporter of the time.

While his career was going well, Dickens's love life was less successful. When he was 17, he had met Maria Beadnell, the pretty and flirtatious daughter of a banker. He fell in love with her. However, her parents were not so keen on any possible relationship between their daughter and a poor shorthand reporter, and they sent Maria to Paris to 'finish her education'. On her return she was cold and indifferent towards him, and he was left to nurse his broken heart and wounded pride. It is likely that this rejection made him all the more determined to succeed in his career and fight his way out of poverty. (An older Maria Beadnell was to reappear as Flora Finching in *Little Dorrit*.)

Charles Dickens at the age of 18, painted by his aunt, Janet Barrow

A page of shorthand written by Dickens. It was very difficult to learn and he later wrote: 'The changes that were wrung upon dots...the wonderful vagaries that were played by circles...not only troubled my waking hours, but reappeared before me in my sleep...'

Marriage and tragedy

In 1834, an editor called George Hogarth asked Dickens to write some sketches for a new paper called the *Evening Chronicle*. Dickens obliged, and soon became a friend of the Hogarth family. He fell in love once more, this time with Hogarth's eldest daughter Catherine. They became engaged, and were married in 1836. By this time, *Sketches by Boz* had been published and *The Pickwick Papers* was becoming a runaway success (see page 16). Dickens was already working furiously to try to fulfil promises made for more sketches, a children's book, a new novel and more – all in addition to his reporting work. This pattern of boundless energy and overwork was to characterise the rest of his life.

Charles and Catherine Dickens started their married life with two permanent lodgers in their London home (now a museum) – Dickens's brother Fred and one of Catherine's sisters, Mary. Mary Hogarth was kind and gentle, and soon became an important part of the household. One night, after returning from the theatre, Mary fell ill quite suddenly and died in Dickens's arms. She was only 17. It was a catastrophe for the whole family, but Dickens took Mary's death extremely badly. The sense of grief and loss was to stay with him for the rest of his life. He himself composed the words for her gravestone: 'Young, beautiful, and good' – words that reappear in later descriptions of female characters in several of his novels.

The title page of *Sketches by Boz* illustrated by George Cruikshank. Cruikshank also illustrated *Oliver Twist*.

> *When he saw her sitting there all alone, so young, and good, and beautiful, and kind to him; and heard her thrilling voice, so natural and sweet, and such a golden link between him and all life's happiness... he turned his face away, and hid his tears.*

Paul Dombey watching his sister, Florence, singing in *Dombey and Son*.

A sketch of Dickens, Catherine Hogarth (centre) and Catherine's sister Mary. Mary's sudden death at the age of 17 devastated Dickens. He based the character of Rose Maylie in *Oliver Twist* on his sister-in-law.

The famous author

Charles Dickens in the gardens of Gad's Hill Place with his two daughters, Mamie and Kate. Another daughter, Dora, died in infancy.

Charles Dickens's fame grew rapidly. He had resigned from his job as a reporter in 1836, and spent all of his time writing plays, sketches, and novels: *Oliver Twist* and *Nicholas Nickleby* appeared from 1837 to 1839, *The Old Curiosity Shop* and *Barnaby Rudge* from 1840 to 1841. He, Catherine and their growing family (by 1841 there were four children) moved to increasingly grand houses, marking Dickens's rise in status. He became well known abroad, too. As a result, in 1842 Dickens decided to visit America. He and Catherine were greeted with rapture by the American public and spent an exhausting six months travelling from one social engagement to another.

Over the next few years, Dickens grew more and more restless. He took his family to Italy to live near Genoa for a year; then after a brief spell back in England they moved to Lausanne in Switzerland, then to Paris. Another favourite retreat was Broadstairs in Kent. All the time he continued to write – *Dombey and Son*, *David Copperfield* and *Bleak House* – as well as finding time to produce his own plays, set up a newspaper and edit a weekly magazine called *Household Words*.

Break-up

It was Gad's Hill Place, the house Dickens bought near Chatham in Kent (see page 6), that provided him with a permanent retreat from 1857 onwards. In the same year, Dickens wrote in a letter to his old friend, John Forster:

> 66 *Poor Catherine and I are not made for each other, and there is no help for it. It is not only that she makes me uneasy and unhappy, but that I make her so too....* 99

After 20 years of marriage he had stopped loving his wife, and found her company intolerable. What is more, Dickens had met a young actress called Ellen Ternan who fascinated him. With her youth and her beauty she reminded him of Mary. After much public argument, Charles and Catherine finally separated in 1858. The children stayed with Charles, except the eldest son Charley, who went with his mother. Catherine's sister, Georgina, who had lived with the family for many years, chose to stay with Dickens. She continued to run his house and care for him until his death.

During the last 12 years of his life Dickens's health grew progressively worse, yet he continued to work just as hard. He undertook long tours of readings from his own works (see page 27). He even returned to America, to great acclaim once more. He continued his relationship with Ellen Ternan, who often visited Gad's Hill Place. Dickens died there on 9 June 1870. Despite his wish to be buried in the graveyard at Rochester Cathedral, the pressure of public opinion persuaded the family to accept a grave in Westminster Cathedral, and he was buried there in Poets' Corner on 14 June.

The actress, Ellen Ternan. When Dickens met Ellen in 1857 she was only 18 – he was 45.

The Staplehurst disaster

In June 1865, Dickens, Ellen Ternan and her mother were travelling back from Paris. They arrived in a steamer at Folkestone harbour and caught the London train. The train was travelling at about 50 miles an hour when the driver suddenly saw a man with a red flag – there was repair work being carried out on the line. He applied the brakes, but it was too late. The train leapt across the gap in the line and its coaches were flung from the track. Dickens and his companions escaped without serious injury, but there were scenes of carnage all around them. From that time onwards, Dickens found it difficult to travel by train, although he forced himself to do so.

A sketch of the wreckage made the day after the Staplehurst railway disaster. The crash killed ten people but Dickens, Ellen and her mother escaped without serious injury.

Serialisation and publication

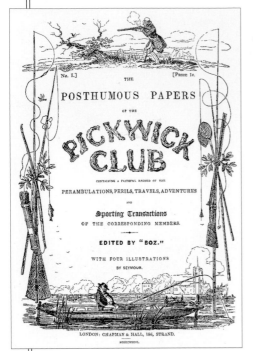

*D*uring his years as a lawyer's clerk and a reporter, Dickens came to know every street and square in London. He spent many hours exploring the city, and observing life in the most squalid, and the grandest, neighbourhoods. He started to put his acute eye and memory to good use with a series of fictional articles, called sketches, about London life and characters. The sketches were first published in 1833 in the *Monthly Magazine*, and were soon attracting comment and praise. He often used the pen-name 'Boz', so when a publisher suggested that the articles should be collected together into a single volume, they came out under the title *Sketches by Boz*. Dickens's first book was published on 7 February 1836, his 24th birthday.

Almost immediately he was invited to write another book – this time it would be serialised in 20 parts. And so *The Pickwick Papers* was born and Dickens's literary career was well and truly started.

This is the cover of the first part of *Pickwick Papers*, price one shilling.

Publishing in parts

All of Dickens's full-length novels were serialised – published in sections of a few chapters at a time – and this contributed to his success as a writer. At that time, novels usually came out in three volumes, which were expensive, meaning that only the middle and upper classes could afford them. By serialising three or four chapters every month at the cost of one shilling, Dickens was able to reach a much wider audience. And because he was

An illustration from the original edition of *Pickwick Papers* published in 1836, which today can be found on the back of a £10 note.

Lending libraries

In 1852 Charles Mudie started a private lending library. Its subscribers paid one guinea (one pound and a shilling) per year to borrow as many books as they could read. Since this was less than the cost of a single new novel, the venture proved very popular. Publishers also benefited from Mudie's enterprise, for it gave them a reliable market for their novels, provided Mudie approved of the content, which had to be appropriate for the whole family. Dickens published the first complete edition of *Great Expectations* in three volumes in order to sell it to Mudie's library.

publishing and writing at the same time, he was able to build up a close relationship with his readers as he went along. The Victorian public responded to his books in the same way that a modern audience reacts to soap operas on television.

Dickens identified with his characters as strongly as his readers. He wrote to a friend about Little Nell in *The Old Curiosity Shop*:

> " *I am slowly murdering that poor child, and grow wretched over it. It wrings my heart. Yet it must be.* "

The method of writing episodes to a tight schedule was extremely demanding – Dickens could not afford to miss the deadline for an instalment – but it clearly suited his energetic character. For example, while he was still writing *The Pickwick Papers* Dickens started to publish *Oliver Twist*, and then no sooner was *The Pickwick Papers* finished than he began work on his next book, *Nicholas Nickleby*. Once the last instalment of each novel was published Dickens then sold it as a complete book, in order to earn the maximum profit from his writing.

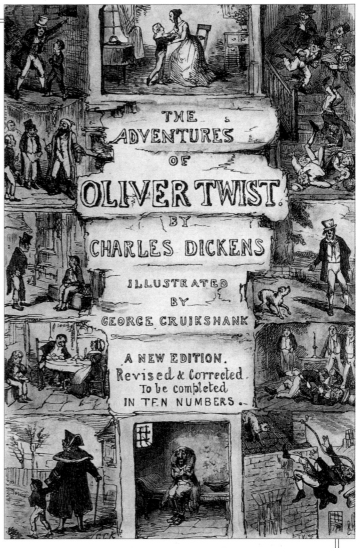

George Cruikshank's title page for *Oliver Twist*, showing scenes from the novel. This edition was serialised in ten parts.

Writing weekly

Dickens wrote several of his novels in weekly instalments. Three were published in the weekly magazines that he edited. *Hard Times* appeared in *Household Words* in 1854 and, although Dickens found the effort of writing to a weekly schedule 'crushing', the book significantly improved the sales of the magazine. *A Tale of Two Cities* and *Great Expectations* were published in the successor to *Household Words*, which Dickens called *All the Year Round*. Bearing in mind the hectic life he was leading at the time, it is perhaps no coincidence that these three are the shortest full-length novels that he wrote.

A letter by Dickens bears witness to his busy lifestyle: 'Tomorrow is a very bad day for me to make a call, as in addition to my usual office business, I have a mass of accounts to settle with Wills…'

Dickens and childhood

Dickens told only one person – his close friend John Forster – about his painful childhood experiences in the blacking factory (see page 10). Nevertheless, he used the memories of his time in the factory and his family's imprisonment in the Marshalsea Prison to create a number of child characters. These fictional children feel similar hurt and confusion and suffer similar misfortunes to those endured by Dickens. However, the energy with which Dickens overcame his own family difficulties and made the most of his opportunities can also be seen in some of his characters. They end up wiser and more tolerant than their own parents and teachers.

The starving boys of Dotheboys Hall as illustrated by 'Phiz' for *Nicholas Nickleby*. 'Phiz' was the illustrator Hablot K. Browne.

The Yorkshire schools

Some of the adults in Dickens's novels are extremely cruel to the children in their care. There was very little protection for children in the 19th century, and schools were often as dangerous as factories or mines for a child. Perhaps the most famous of Dickens's fictional schools is Dotheboys Hall, in *Nicholas Nickleby*, run by the headmaster Wackford Squeers.

> *But the pupils – the young noblemen!...There were little faces which should have been handsome, darkened with the scowl of sullen suffering; there was childhood with the light of its eye quenched, its beauty gone, and its helplessness alone remaining; there were vicious boys brooding, with leaden eyes, like malefactors in a jail...*
>
> Dickens's description of the pupils at Dotheboys Hall

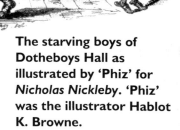

Dotheboys Hall is based on real-life schools in Yorkshire where children were abandoned to a brutal life – and sometimes death. In 1838, Dickens visited Yorkshire to research *Nicholas Nickleby*, travelling under an assumed name to avoid recognition. He met a headmaster called William Shaw and later wrote in his diary: 'Shaw the schoolmaster we saw today, is the man in whose school several boys went blind sometime since, from gross neglect...'

Wackford Squeers, the headmaster of Dotheboys Hall

Cruelty at home

Home was not necessarily a safer place to be. Pip, the hero of *Great Expectations*, is beaten regularly by his sister, Mrs Joe Gargery, who brings him up 'by hand' with the cane which she calls 'Tickler'. She also pours a disgusting medicine known as 'tar-water' down his throat as a punishment. *David Copperfield* includes a character familiar in many stories of childhood: the evil step-parent. In this novel, it is Edward Murdstone who marries David's vulnerable mother and victimises David. David retaliates finally by biting his hand, and receives a vicious flogging in return. Mr Murdstone packs him off to a boarding school, Salem House, where he is made to wear a sign which reads: 'Take care of him. He bites.'

The convict, Magwitch, confronts Pip at the beginning of a television adaptation of *Great Expectations*.

On the streets

The time Dickens spent on the streets of London as a young boy is recalled in several novels. *Oliver Twist* has many scenes involving child pickpockets who scratch a living either for themselves or for a gangleader – in Oliver's case the cunning villain, Fagin.

One of the saddest characters in all of Dickens's work is Jo, the crossing sweeper in *Bleak House*. He earns money by keeping a clear path across the busy and filthy main road, and although he has compassion for others, he lives a miserable and lonely life.

Dickens sums up Jo's empty and ignorant existence in *Bleak House*:

66 *Name, Jo. Nothing else that he knows on. Don't know that everybody has two names. Never heerd of sich a think. Don't know that Jo is short for a longer name. Thinks it long enough for him… Spell it? No. He can't spell it. No father, no mother, no friends. Never been to school. What's home?* 99

Fagin inspects his ill-gotten wealth in the film/musical version of *Oliver Twist*.

Dickens and Christmas

*I*n 1843, Dickens found that he was not earning enough to support his growing family. So he tried a new venture to improve his income. This was a short book intended to make the most of the increasingly popular market for Christmas annuals.

A Christmas Carol

Dickens wrote *A Christmas Carol* in the space of six weeks. He worked with such speed and energy that he later said he wept and laughed and wandered the streets of London 'fifteen and twenty miles many a night when all sober folks had gone to bed'. The book was published in November 1843 and the whole of the first edition of 6000 copies was sold on the first day. Booksellers ordered 2000 more copies even before they could be printed.

Dickens was particularly anxious that the book should be of a high quality, including four colour illustrations, and he paid for the production himself. Although the book was a great success, he was horrified to discover from his publishers that his initial royalties amounted to only £230, which was much less than he had hoped.

A Christmas Carol has always been one of the most popular of all Dickens's books, and it has many of the typical features of his full-length novels. Scrooge, the grim old miser; Tiny Tim, the disabled boy full of concern for others; the contrast between the sordid streets of London and the strong, supportive families of Bob Cratchit and Mr Fezziwig, are some of the ingredients of its appeal. But most important of all is the fairytale way that everything turns out for the best, which readers have associated with the spirit of Christmas.

Mr Fezziwig's Ball, one of the four full colour illustrations by John Leech that appeared in the first edition of *A Christmas Carol*. Fezziwig's generosity as an employer contrasts with Scrooge's mean treatment of Bob Cratchit.

In *A Christmas Carol*, Scrooge is taken to watch the Fezziwig family and friends enjoying their Christmas party:

> *There were more dances, and there were forfeits, and more dances, and there was cake, and there was negus [a hot alcoholic drink], and there was a great piece of Cold Roast, and there was a great piece of Cold Boiled, and there were mince-pies, and plenty of beer...*

Christmas books

Hoping to repeat the success of *A Christmas Carol*, Dickens wrote several more Christmas books. In 1844, while he was living in Genoa, he wrote *The Chimes*. The central character of this book is a poor man called Toby (Trotty) Veck. He falls asleep on New Year's Eve, worrying about his daughter and her fiancé, and has a dream in which he sees the dangers of poverty and prostitution. However, he wakes up on New Year's Day with the hopeful sound of bells ringing in his ears. Dickens returned to England in order to read *The Chimes* to a group of friends before Christmas. They were very moved by it, and when it was published it immediately sold 20,000 copies and proved to be a better commercial success than *A Christmas Carol*.

Dickens wrote three more Christmas books. *The Cricket on the Hearth* was the most popular of all of them when it was first published in 1845. But he found *The Battle of Life* (1846) and *The Haunted Man* (1847) very difficult to write, and after 1847 he wrote Christmas stories only on a much smaller scale.

The Spirits of the Bells.

'The Spirits of the Bells', one of the engravings by Daniel Maclise for Dickens's Christmas book *The Chimes*

Dickens reads *The Chimes* to a group of friends in December 1844. The group includes his brother Fred, the illustrator Daniel Maclise, and his lifelong friend John Forster.

Dickens the reformer

*A*lthough Dickens usually had at least one novel in the process of serialisation, he remained a busy journalist and editor at the same time as writing fiction. In March 1850 he started up a weekly magazine called *Household Words* in order to air the social issues about which he felt very strongly, such as legal and prison reform, poverty and housing for the poor, education, crime and the conditions of factory workers.

Most of his early books contain some social comment. For example, anyone reading *Oliver Twist* was bound to be appalled by the dreadful slum conditions in which the petty criminals of the novel live. In *A Christmas Carol* Dickens pointedly drew attention to the misery of the poor by naming two of the little children Want and Ignorance. By the 1850s, however, Dickens was more impatient with society and his novels of this period are much more direct in their attack on various institutions.

An engraving by Gustave Doré showing the homeless poor of London applying for help at a refuge. The plight of the poor was a constant theme in Dickens's novels.

Fog everywhere

The opening pages of *Bleak House* are a masterpiece of atmospheric writing. Dickens makes the fog hanging over London represent the murky and stifling force of the law and the traditions of wealth and power that protect it. In the novel, Dickens attacks the wasteful practices of the law courts and highlights the conditions of the poorest people living among the slums and graveyards of London.

Dense, choking fog fills a busy London street in 1867.

> **"** *Fog everywhere. Fog up the river, where it flows among green aits [small islands] and meadows; fog down the river, where it rolls defiled among the tiers of shipping, and the waterside pollutions of a great (and dirty) city. Fog on the Essex Marshes, fog on the Kentish heights.* **"**
>
> *Bleak House*

In the same way that Dickens visited Yorkshire while planning *Nicholas Nickleby* (see page 18), he arranged a trip in 1854 to Preston, Lancashire, to observe at first hand the effects of the Industrial Revolution on the mill workers. When he returned to London he started work on his next novel, *Hard Times*. It was to be his shortest novel (partly because he wrote it in weekly instalments for *Household Words*) and one in which there is very little humour. The particular object of his attack in *Hard Times* is the lack of interest of the mill-owners in the welfare of their employees. Dickens paints a picture of society in which nothing is valued unless it can be used to make money. As a result family life, love and imagination are all cruelly suppressed.

Angela Burdett-Coutts

Angela Burdett-Coutts (right) was a rich heiress who inherited two vast fortunes. She decided to use her wealth to help the poor, and relied on Dickens for advice on how and where her money should be spent. She supported the Ragged Schools (see page 9), paid for a model housing scheme in Bethnal Green, and set up a house for reformed prostitutes and female offenders. She became a close friend of the Dickens family, although she and Dickens drew apart after his separation from Catherine.

The opening words of *Hard Times* establish the grim mood of the novel:

> *Now, what I want is, Facts. Teach these boys and girls nothing but Facts. Facts alone are wanted in life. Plant nothing else, and root out everything else. You can only form the minds of reasoning animals upon Facts: nothing else will ever be of any service to them... Stick to Facts, sir!*

Little Dorrit

In the third of his novels to be written in the heat of his desire to bring about reform, Dickens returned to one of the most powerful influences on his own life: the Marshalsea Prison. *Little Dorrit* (written in monthly parts between 1855 and 1857) is about many different aspects of imprisonment, both physical and mental. The heroine's father, William Dorrit, has spent 25 years in the Marshalsea Prison, and has been so affected by his time there that he has become almost a different person. One of Dickens's more notable creations in the novel is the Circumlocution Office, which, like the law courts in *Bleak House*, is the kind of faceless, inflexible, inhuman institution that Dickens most wanted to do away with.

Amy Dorrit ('Little Dorrit') sits in her garret room in the Marshalsea Prison. Born and brought up in the prison, she eventually marries a Marshalsea prisoner, Arthur Clenham.

Dickens as hero

> *Whether I shall turn out to be the hero of my own life, or whether that station will be held by anybody else these pages must show.*

With these words Dickens began the novel which, more than any other, revealed his own character and experience. *David Copperfield* (begun in February 1849 and finished in October 1850) is written as a fictional autobiography. The character of David relates the story of his childhood and growth into maturity, but in many respects Dickens was re-writing his own life story. For example, after his mother has died David is forced by his step-father, Edward Murdstone, to work in a warehouse, washing and labelling wine bottles – recalling Dickens's own experiences in the blacking factory.

David describes his feelings as he is put to work in the bottling warehouse:

> *I mingled my tears with the water in which I was washing the bottles; and sobbed as if there were a flaw in my own breast, and it were in danger of bursting.*

David Copperfield meets Mr Micawber in a film version of *David Copperfield*. One of Mr Micawber's philosophies of life is that something will always 'turn up'.

Real-life characters

The character of Mr Micawber, which Dickens took great care in creating, is very close to that of Dickens's own father. Mr Micawber spends some time in prison – the King's Bench Prison, not far from the Marshalsea Prison where John Dickens was sent. He is an eternal optimist, moving from one temporary job to the next.

Dickens also worked into the story his youthful love for Maria Beadnell (see page 12). She is represented by Dora Spenlow, the childish and impractical daughter of David's employer, who is a lawyer in London. In real life Dickens was rejected by Maria, but in the novel David marries Dora. She later dies in childbirth, and David marries again, this time to Agnes Wickfield. Agnes has many of the characteristics of Dickens's sister-in-law, Georgina (see page 15), whom Dickens admired for her efficiency and goodness.

Mr Micawber, from a television adaptation of *David Copperfield*.

Great Expectations

David Copperfield was written in the middle of Dickens's career. In one of his last novels, *Great Expectations* (written between December 1860 and August 1861), he returned again to his childhood – but this was a very different kind of novel. Indeed, Dickens re-read *David Copperfield* before starting *Great Expectations* to make sure he was not going to repeat any of the same material. Dickens set the first section of the book in the part of Kent where he spent the happiest years of his childhood, in the marshes north of Chatham and in Rochester. *Great Expectations* is also a fictional autobiography, but Dickens avoided any factual similarities with his own life, instead communicating very powerfully his own feelings and attitudes.

By this time he had bought the house at Gad's Hill Place (see page 6), and enjoyed the kind of lifestyle and fame that he could only have dreamed of when he and his father first walked past the house all those years ago. But the theme of the novel is the discovery that money and genteel society are worthless compared to honest, simple human kindness.

The 13 lozenge-shaped graves of the children of the Comport family lie in Cooling churchyard, Kent. Dickens often walked to Cooling from Gad's Hill Place, and he used Cooling as the setting for the opening of *Great Expectations*.

Who did not know him?

John Harmon and Bella in a recent television adaptation of *Our Mutual Friend*.

Dickens's fame in his own lifetime cannot be over-emphasised. He was a media star, and as well-known to the Victorian public as any television personality is today. His books appealed to people of all classes. And the method of their publication (see page 16) ensured that they were affordable by a larger audience than any previous books.

> *He was to be seen, by those who knew him, everywhere – and who did not know him? Who had not heard him read, and who had not seen his photograph in the shop-windows? The omnibus-conductors knew him, the street boys knew him...*
>
> Philip Collins *Interviews and Recollections* Macmillan 1981

Dickens holds an audience enthralled on one of his many reading tours. The tours were a great success, but they took a terrible toll on Dickens's already failing health.

Social changes also played a part in Dickens's appeal. For many people, the Industrial Revolution had brought an increase in standards of living. More people were literate, and many middle class people, especially women, had more leisure time than ever before. There were also practical developments in the home, such as improved lighting, which made reading easier. In many homes, the latest instalment of Dickens's novels would be read aloud to an enthralled audience.

Of course, not everything Dickens wrote or did was greeted with approval. Some of his novels did not sell as well as others, and reviews of his books were sometimes less than complimentary. Henry James wrote of *Our Mutual Friend*: 'It were, in our opinion, an offence against humanity to place Mr Dickens among the greatest novelists... He has added nothing to our understanding of human character.' Dickens was also aware of the need to protect his public image, in order to maintain his popularity. When he and his wife separated he was greatly concerned that the scandal might affect his ability to earn money and support his large family (there were nine Dickens children; a tenth died as a baby). He even published a personal statement in *Household Words* to try to dispel the rumours that were being spread about him and Catherine.

Beyond his lifetime

Dickens's influence and fame has extended well beyond his own lifetime. The novelist George Gissing, who also wrote about the poor and deprived of Britain's industrial cities, acknowledged his debt to Dickens. Dickens's books were popular in Russia from the 1840s onwards: both Fyodor Dostoevsky and Leo Tolstoy, author of *War and Peace*, were heavily influenced by Dickens's writing. Tolstoy even learned English so that he could read Dickens's books in their original language.

The potential for adapting Dickens's novels for the stage was realised by the author himself. He often helped with dramatisations of his novels, or episodes from his novels. The practice has continued ever since, with stage versions such as *The Life and Adventures of Nicholas Nickleby*, film adaptations including David Lean's *Great Expectations*, musicals such as *Oliver!* and many television adaptations. Today, Dickens's world continues to live for us on the stage and screen and, just like those first readers over 100 years ago, in the words on the page.

Pip (Michael York) and Miss Havisham (Margaret Leighton) in a 1975 film of *Great Expectations*

Dramatic readings

Towards the end of his life, Dickens undertook several reading tours. He travelled the British Isles, Ireland and America, enthralling audiences with readings from his own works. His talents as an actor are obvious in the descriptions of the hypnotic effect he had on the huge audiences that flocked to see him. He wrote of an audience in Ireland: 'I have never seen men go in to cry so undisguisedly as they did at that reading yesterday afternoon.' As usual, Dickens was concerned to reach as wide an audience as possible and ensured that tickets were available at all prices: 'The stalls are five shillings, but I have made them fix the working men's admissions at threepence...'

CHARLES DICKENS

WILL READ AT THE

FESTIVAL CONCERT ROOM,

YORK,

ON

MONDAY EVENING,

OCTOBER 25th, at 8 o'Clock.

THE POOR TRAVELLER,

BOOTS AT THE **HOLLY TREE INN,**

AND

MRS. GAMP.

PLACES FOR THE READING		
Stalls, (numbered and reserved)	-	Four Shillings.
Gallery,	-	Two Shillings.
Back Seats,	-	One Shilling.

Tickets to be had of Mr. HENRY BANKS, Music Warehouse, Stonegate, York,

Where a Plan of the Reserved Seats may be seen.

THE READING WILL LAST TWO HOURS

A poster for one of Dickens's readings in York. Note that the ticket prices range from one to four shillings.

HISTORICAL EVENTS		DICKENS'S LIFE
Luddite attacks on mills	**1812**	Charles John Huffam Dickens born 7 February in Landport, Portsmouth
Defeat of Napoleon by Wellington at Waterloo. Corn Law passed by British Parliament to protect price of wheat	**1815**	Catherine Hogarth, later Charles Dickens's wife, is born
	1817	Dickens family moves to Chatham, Kent. Charles Dickens goes to school
Peterloo Massacre of Corn Law protestors. Factory Act protects child workers in cotton factories	**1819**	
	1822	Dickens family moves to London
	1823	Charles Dickens goes to work at Warren's blacking factory
	1824	John Dickens is arrested for debt and imprisoned in Marshalsea Prison
Opening of Stockton-Darlington railway	**1825**	
	1827	Charles Dickens leaves school and starts work in a lawyer's office
Robert Peel, Home Secretary, founds the Metropolitan Police in London	**1829**	
George IV dies, succeeded by William IV. Opening of Liverpool to Manchester railway	**1830**	Dickens meets Maria Beadnell
	1831	Dickens starts work as a reporter for the *Mirror of Parliament*
Reform Act reorganises voting system and parliamentary seats	**1832**	Dickens becomes a reporter for *The True Sun*
Factory Act limits working day for nine-to 13-year-olds to nine hours	**1833**	Romance with Maria Beadnell ends. First story published in the *Monthly Magazine*
	1835	Series of sketches published in the *Evening Chronicle*
	1836	*Sketches by Boz* is published. First instalment of *The Pickwick Papers* published. Dickens marries Catherine Hogarth
William IV dies, succeeded by Victoria	**1837**	First child, Charles (Charley), born. *Oliver Twist* starts publication.
Anti-Corn Law League founded in Manchester. London to Birmingham Railway, and Euston Station in London, open	**1838**	Dickens travels to Yorkshire to research schools. Second child Mary (Mamie) born. *Nicholas Nickleby* starts publication
	1839	Third child, Kate, born
Marriage of Queen Victoria and Prince Albert Saxe-Coburg.	**1840**	*The Old Curiosity Shop* starts publication
	1841	Fourth child, Walter, born. *Barnaby Rudge* published

HISTORICAL EVENTS		DICKENS'S LIFE
	1842	Dickens and Catherine tour America. *American Notes* published
Launch of S.S. *Great Britain*, the first iron-hulled ocean-going ship	**1843**	*The Life and Adventures of Martin Chuzzlewit* starts publication. *A Christmas Carol* published
Factory Act restricts female workers to a 12-hour day and children to 6.5 hours. Ragged Schools are founded	**1844**	Fifth child, Francis, born. Dickens family in Italy. *The Chimes* published
	1845	Sixth child, Alfred, born. *The Cricket on the Hearth* published
	1846	Dickens launches newspaper *Daily News*. Dickens family in Switzerland and Paris. *Dombey and Son* begins publication. *The Battle of Life* published. *Pictures from Italy* published
	1847	Seventh child, Sydney, born. Last Christmas book, *The Haunted Man*, published
Chartist movement collapses after mass meeting in London	**1848**	
	1849	Eighth child, Henry, born. *David Copperfield* begins publication
Factory Act defines legal working hours	**1850**	*Household Words* begins weekly publication. Ninth child, Dora, born
Cholera epidemic in Britain	**1852**	*Bleak House* starts publication. Tenth child, Edward (Plorn), born
Crimean War (until 1856)	**1854**	*Hard Times* starts publication
	1855	*Little Dorrit* starts publication
	1856	Dickens buys Gad's Hill Place in Kent
Indian Mutiny	**1857**	Dickens meets Ellen Ternan
	1858	Dickens and Catherine separate
Darwin's *Origin of Species* published	**1859**	Dickens starts a new weekly magazine *All The Year Round*. *A Tale of Two Cities* starts publication
	1860	*Great Expectations* starts publication
	1864	*Our Mutual Friend* starts publication
	1865	Dickens and Ellen Ternan are involved in the Staplehurst railway accident
	1867-8	Dickens tours America, giving public readings
	1870	*The Mystery of Edwin Drood* starts publication but is left unfinished at Dickens's death. Dickens dies 9 June.

Index

Further reading:

A Charles Dickens Selection edited by Peter Thomas, Heinemann

Who's Who in Dickens by Donald Hawes, Routledge

History in Literature: The Story behind Charles Dickens' Oliver Twist by Brian Williams, Heinemann

Places and websites to visit

Dickens House Museum, 48 Doughty Street, London, WC1N 2LF (Dickens' home 1837 – 1839) http://www.dickensmuseum.com/. Go to http://www.dickensmuseum.com/vtour/ for a virtual tour of the museum.

Dickens' Birthplace, 393, Old Commercial Road, Portsmouth, Hants http://www.charlesdickensbirthplace.co.uk/

Dickens World, Leviathan Way, Chatham Maritime, Kent ME4 4LL http://www.dickensworld.co.uk/

http://www.victorianweb.org/authors/dickens/index.html Literature, culture and history in the age of Victoria

http://www.bbc.co.uk/history/historic_figures/dickens_charles.shtml BBC site about Dickens